EARTH'S HEMISPHERES

WESTERN

EASTERN

By Todd Bluthenthal

Gareth Stevens
PUBLISHING

Please visit our website, www.garethstevens.com. For a free color catalog of all our high-quality books, call toll free 1-800-542-2595 or fax 1-877-542-2596.

Cataloging-in-Publication Data

Names: Bluthenthal, Todd.
Title: Earth's hemispheres / Todd Bluthenthal.
Description: New York : Gareth Stevens Publishing, 2017. | Series: Where on Earth? mapping parts of the world | Includes index.
Identifiers: ISBN 9781482464177 (pbk.) | ISBN 9781482464191 (library bound) | ISBN 9781482464184 (6 pack)
Subjects: LCSH: Latitude–Juvenile literature. | Longitude–Juvenile literature. | Geographical positions–Juvenile literature.
Classification: LCC QB224.5 B58 2017 | DDC 526'.61–dc23

Published in 2018 by
Gareth Stevens Publishing
111 East 14th Street, Suite 349
New York, NY 10003

Copyright © 2018 Gareth Stevens Publishing

Designer: Samantha DeMartin
Editor: Joan Stoltman

Photo credits: series art CHAPLIA YAROSLAV/Shutterstock.com; cover, p. 1 Potapov Alexander/Shutterstock.com; p. 5 all_about_people/Shutterstock.com; pp. 7, 9 NoPainNoGain/Shutterstock.com; pp. 11, 13, 15, 17, 19 intrepix/Shutterstock.com; p. 21 (top) 1000 Words/Shutterstock.com; p. 21 (bottom) Li Hui Chen/Shutterstock.com.

Printed in the United States of America

CPSIA compliance information: Batch #CS17GS: For further information contact Gareth Stevens, New York, New York at 1-800-542-2595.

CONTENTS

Boldface words appear in the glossary.

All About Hemispheres!

People put imaginary lines on maps and **globes** to help us find places on Earth. These lines **divide** Earth into hemispheres. "Hemi" means "half," and "sphere" means "globe." So "hemisphere" means "half of a globe"!

The imaginary lines are called latitude and longitude lines. Latitude lines run east and west. They show how far north or south a place is. Longitude lines run north and south. They show how far east or west a place is.

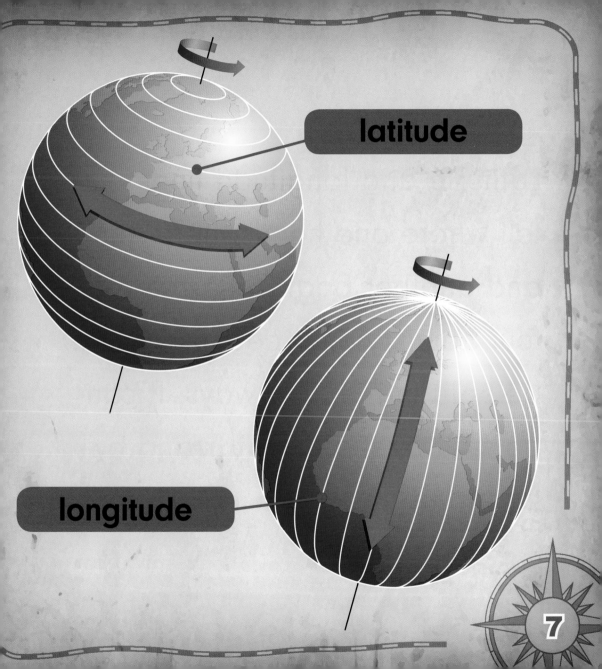

latitude

longitude

Latitude and longitude lines also tell where one hemisphere ends and another begins. Earth has four hemispheres because it can be **split** in half two ways. It can be split by the **equator** and by the **prime meridian**.

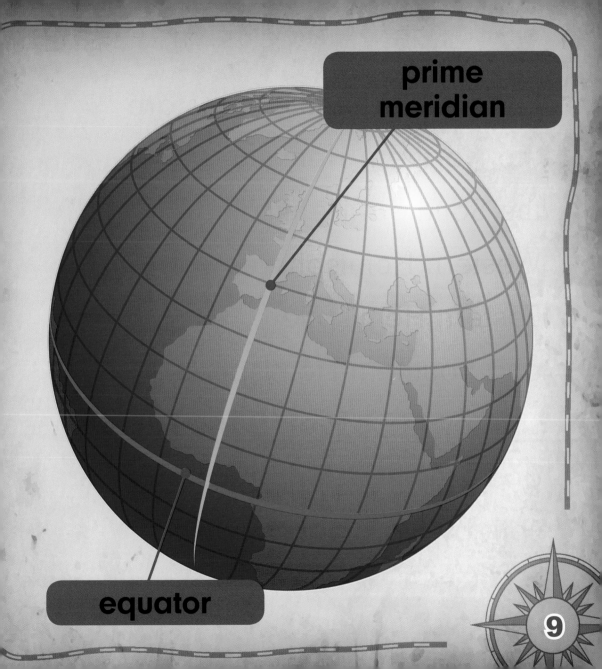

prime
meridian

equator

9

Earth's four hemispheres are the Northern Hemisphere, the Southern Hemisphere, the Western Hemisphere, and the Eastern Hemisphere. The Northern and Southern Hemispheres are split by the equator. The Eastern and Western Hemispheres are split by the prime meridian.

The Northern Hemisphere

The Northern Hemisphere is the half of Earth north of the equator. Europe and North America are only in the Northern Hemisphere. The equator runs through South America, Africa, and Asia. This means only part of those **continents** is in the Northern Hemisphere.

The Southern Hemisphere

The Southern Hemisphere is the half of Earth south of the equator. Australia and Antarctica are only in the Southern Hemisphere. Most of South America is too. In the Southern Hemisphere, summer is from December to March. Wacky!

SOUTH
AMERICA

AFRICA

EQUATOR

AUSTRALIA

INDIAN
OCEAN

SOUTHERN OCEAN

ANTARCTICA

15

The Western Hemisphere

The part of Earth west of the prime meridian is called the Western Hemisphere. It's made up of all North and South America and half of Antarctica. About one-third of all the land of Earth is in the Western Hemisphere.

The Eastern Hemisphere

The Eastern Hemisphere is east of the prime meridian. All Asia and Australia, most of Africa and Europe, and half of Antarctica are in the Eastern Hemisphere. The Eastern Hemisphere has about two-thirds of Earth's land.

EUROPE

ASIA

PACIFIC
OCEAN

AFRICA

PRIME MERIDIAN

AUSTRALIA

INDIAN
OCEAN

SOUTHERN OCEAN

ANTARCTICA

19

How Many People Live There?

Almost 90 **percent** of Earth's **population** live in the Northern Hemisphere! That's because almost all of Earth's land is north of the equator. What hemisphere do you live in?

20

Many people live in the Asian city of Bangkok!

No one lives in Antarctica!

21

GLOSSARY

continent: one of Earth's seven great landmasses

divide: to break up

equator: the main line of latitude that runs east and west

globe: a ball, like Earth

percent: a small part of a whole

population: the number of people who live in an area

prime meridian: the main line of longitude that runs north and south

split: broken apart

FOR MORE INFORMATION

BOOKS

National Geographic Society. *National Geographic Kids Beginner's World Atlas*. Washington, DC: National Geographic, 2011.

Olien, Rebecca. *Longitude and Latitude*. New York, NY: Children's Press, 2013.

Waldron, Melanie. *Mapping the World*. Chicago, IL: Capstone Raintree, 2012.

WEBSITES

Around the World
timeforkids.com/around-the-world
Travel around the world—through your computer!

Global Trek
teacher.scholastic.com/activities/globaltrek/
Keep a travel journal of the countries you visit here.

Map Maker 2.0 – Make Your Own USA, World and Nation Maps
mrnussbaum.com/mapbuilder2/
Test your new knowledge of the world through mapmaking.

Publisher's note to educators and parents: Our editors have carefully reviewed these websites to ensure that they are suitable for students. Many websites change frequently, however, and we cannot guarantee that a site's future contents will continue to meet our high standards of quality and educational value. Be advised that students should be closely supervised whenever they access the Internet.

INDEX